DOGS AT WORK

SERVICE DOGS

BY JESSICA COUPÉ

WWW.APEXEDITIONS.COM

Copyright © 2023 by Apex Editions, Mendota Heights, MN 55120. All rights reserved. No part of this book may be reproduced or utilized in any form or by any means without written permission from the publisher.

Apex is distributed by North Star Editions:
sales@northstareditions.com | 888-417-0195

Produced for Apex by Red Line Editorial.

Photographs ©: Shutterstock Images, cover, 1, 4–5, 8–9, 10–11, 12–13, 18, 20, 21, 22–23; iStockphoto, 6, 7, 16–17, 24, 25, 26, 29; Tom Sherlin/The Daily Times/AP Images, 15

Library of Congress Control Number: 2022912280

ISBN
978-1-63738-425-1 (hardcover)
978-1-63738-452-7 (paperback)
978-1-63738-505-0 (ebook pdf)
978-1-63738-479-4 (hosted ebook)

Printed in the United States of America
Mankato, MN
012023

NOTE TO PARENTS AND EDUCATORS

Apex books are designed to build literacy skills in striving readers. Exciting, high-interest content attracts and holds readers' attention. The text is carefully leveled to allow students to achieve success quickly. Additional features, such as bolded glossary words for difficult terms, help build comprehension.

TABLE OF CONTENTS

CHAPTER 1
HEADING HOME 4

CHAPTER 2
HELPING HUMANS 10

CHAPTER 3
ON THE JOB 16

CHAPTER 4
TRAINING 22

COMPREHENSION QUESTIONS • 28
GLOSSARY • 30
TO LEARN MORE • 31
ABOUT THE AUTHOR • 31
INDEX • 32

CHAPTER 1

HEADING HOME

A boy is going home from school. He uses a wheelchair. He has a service dog, too. The dog helps him ride the bus to his apartment.

Some service dogs help their owners ride on buses or trains.

An elevator's buttons may be hard for some people to press or reach.

Inside the building, the boy takes an elevator. His dog pushes the buttons for him. Later, she helps him open his apartment door.

FAST FACT

Service dogs can press doorbells and crosswalk buttons.

Service dogs can carry or pick up objects for their owners.

Mobility assistance dogs can tug on ropes to open gates and doors.

8

The dog flips a switch to turn on the lights. Then she pulls the door shut.

MANY MOVEMENTS

Mobility assistance dogs help people who have limited movement. The dogs can open doors and drawers. They can pick up dropped items. Some bring their owners medicine, too.

CHAPTER 2

HELPING HUMANS

Service dogs are trained to help people with **disabilities**. There are several types of service dogs. Each type does different tasks.

Some service dogs assist people who use wheelchairs.

Guide dogs watch for things their owners can't see.

Guide dogs work with people who cannot see. They help people get from one place to another.

FAST FACT

Dogs may bark or lick to alert their owners.

Hearing dogs help deaf people. They listen for sounds and *alert* their owners.

Medical alert dogs warn people when a problem is about to happen. Some dogs smell **allergens**. Others help people who have **seizures** or **diabetes**. The dogs' warnings help these people stay safe.

AUTISM SERVICE DOGS

Some service dogs help **autistic** people. When people feel stressed or upset, their dogs can nudge or cuddle them. This helps them feel calmer.

By smelling problems before they happen, medical alert dogs give people time to prepare.

15

CHAPTER 3

ON THE JOB

Service dogs live with their owners. They help with tasks around the home. Owners also bring them to work or school.

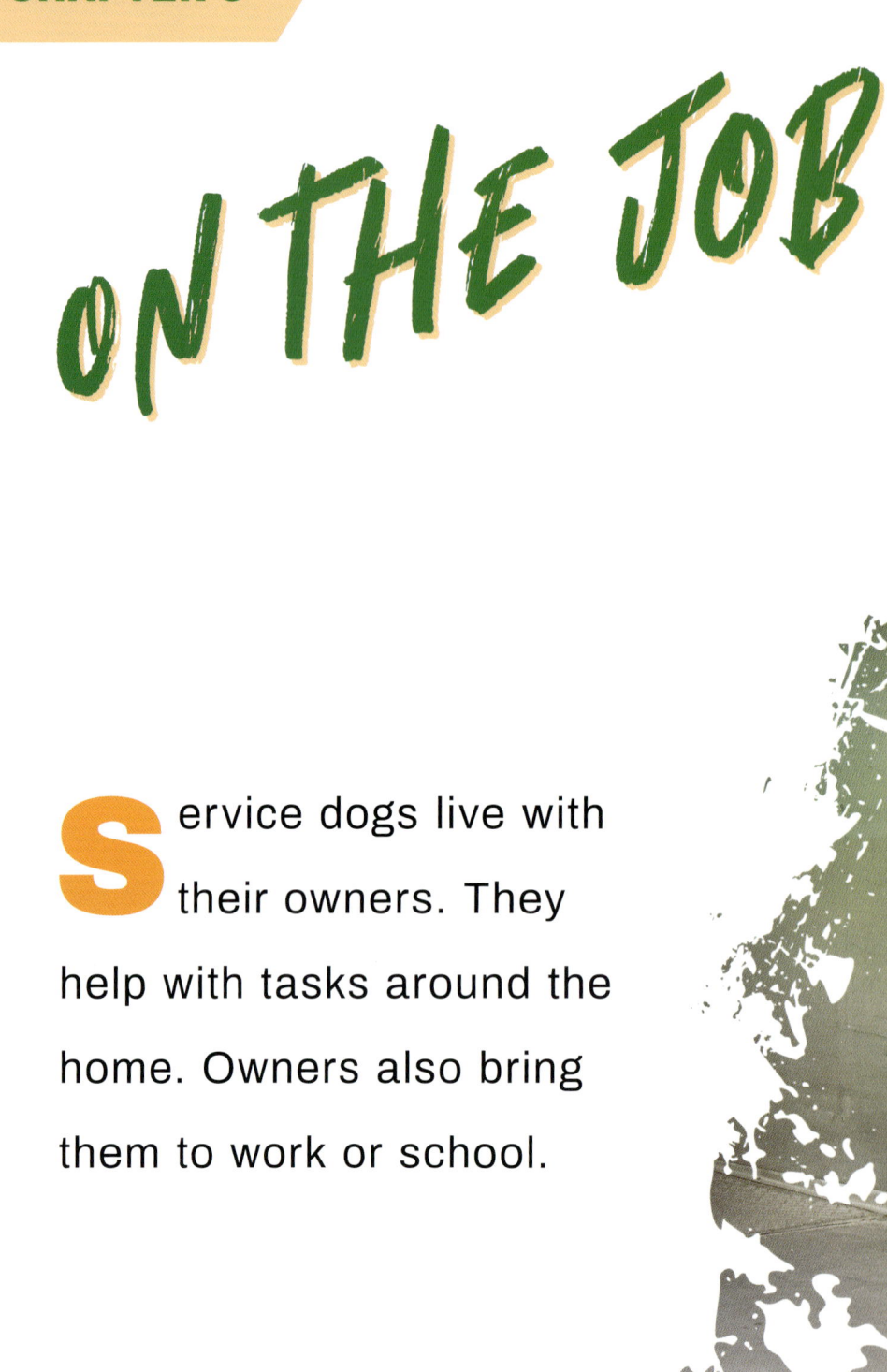

Service dogs make it easier for their owners to go about their daily lives.

18

In fact, service dogs go everywhere their owners do. They ride on trains and airplanes. And they visit restaurants and stores.

FAST FACT
Because they go many places, service dogs must be friendly and calm.

Service dogs learn to wait quietly when they are out and about.

Vests help people know not to pet or distract service dogs while they're working.

Service dogs often wear a vest and a harness. The vest shows people that the dog is working. It's not just a pet. So, it's allowed to go more places.

DIFFERENT BREEDS

Mobility assistance dogs may pull wheelchairs or move people. So, they're often big breeds, such as German shepherds. Medical alert dogs need strong noses. They may be smaller.

Pomeranians are tiny. But they can be medical alert or hearing dogs.

CHAPTER 4

TRAINING

Service dogs start training when they are puppies. Puppies live with trainers for a year. The trainers bring them to public places, such as stores. This helps the dogs learn to stay calm.

Service dog training usually takes about two years.

By training in different places, dogs get used to many sights and sounds.

Next, dogs attend obedience school. They learn basic **commands** such as "come" and "stay." Dogs practice doing these skills in different places.

FAST FACT

Many service dogs learn more than 30 commands.

Trainers give dogs treats to help them learn.

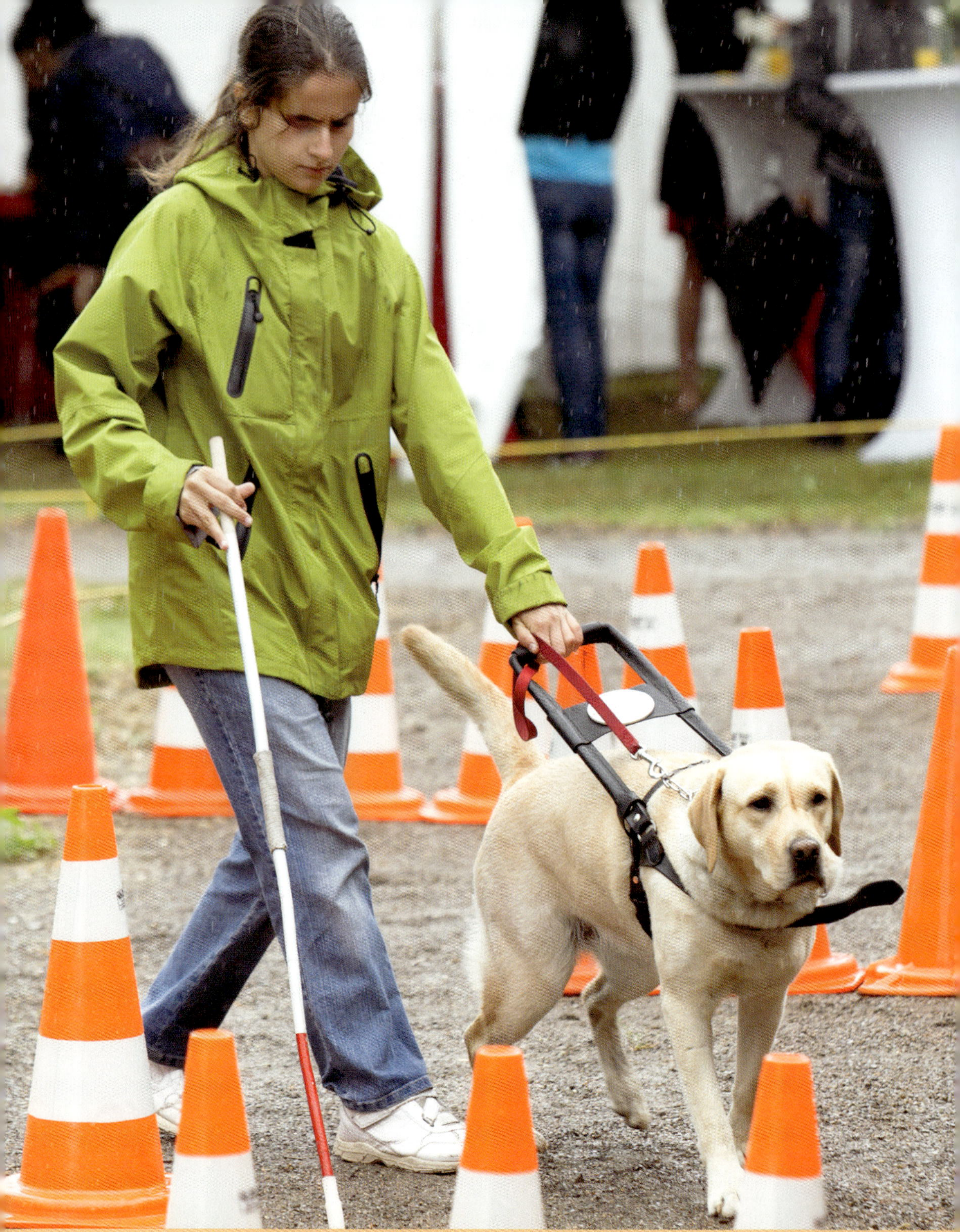

Next, dogs train for a specific job. Guide dogs learn directions. Hearing dogs practice alerting people. After this training, dogs are ready to work.

TRICKY TRAINING

Service dog training is very difficult. Between 50 and 70 percent of dogs do not pass. These dogs are often adopted as pets.

◀ Guide dogs learn commands for turning left or right.

COMPREHENSION QUESTIONS

Write your answers on a separate piece of paper.

1. Write a few sentences that explain the main ideas of Chapter 2.

2. Would you like to train a service dog? Why or why not?

3. Which type of service dog is trained to smell problems and warn its owner?

   A. guide dog
   B. medical alert dog
   C. mobility assistance dog

4. Which type of service dog might learn commands for stopping and turning?

   A. guide dog
   B. hearing dog
   C. autism service dog

5. What does **obedience** mean in this book?

Next, dogs attend obedience school. They learn basic commands such as "come" and "stay."

    A. learning to follow commands
    B. learning to stop moving
    C. learning to read

6. What does **public** mean in this book?

Puppies live with trainers for a year. The trainers bring them to public places, such as stores.

    A. inside a house
    B. where no people can go
    C. where many people can go

Answer key on page 32.

GLOSSARY

alert
To let someone know something is happening.

allergens
Things the body reacts to in a way that makes a person sick.

autistic
Having a condition that affects how a person thinks and communicates.

breeds
Specific types of dogs that have their own looks and abilities.

commands
Ways of telling a dog what to do.

diabetes
A disease that causes problems with a person's blood sugar.

disabilities
Limits or differences in a person's senses or movement.

mobility assistance
Helping people to walk, move, or balance.

seizures
Changes in the brain that cause shaking or other problems.

TO LEARN MORE

BOOKS

Finke, Beth. *Service Dogs*. Ann Arbor, MI: Cherry Lake Publishing, 2022.

Jones, Dale. *Service Dogs*. Minneapolis: Bearport Publishing, 2022.

Laughlin, Kara L. *Seizure-Alert Dogs*. New York: AV2 by Weigl, 2019.

ONLINE RESOURCES

Visit www.apexeditions.com to find links and resources related to this title.

ABOUT THE AUTHOR

Jessica Coupé is the author of several children's books. When not writing, she is learning about her ancestors' stories. She lives in British Columbia, Canada.

INDEX

A
allergens, 14
autism service dogs, 14

B
breeds, 21

C
commands, 24–25

D
deaf, 13
diabetes, 14

G
guide dogs, 12, 27

H
harness, 20
hearing dogs, 13, 27

M
medical alert dogs, 14, 21
mobility assistance dogs, 9, 21

S
school, 4, 16, 24
seizures, 14
stores, 19, 22

T
training, 22, 27

V
vest, 20

W
wheelchairs, 4, 21

ANSWER KEY:
1. Answers will vary; 2. Answers will vary; 3. B; 4. A; 5. A; 6. C